This book aims to help beginners play the French horn. The book includes 45 diagrams with fingering positions and staff notation for 3 different types of French horn. The musical notes cover almost 6 octaves.

The most basic type of French horn (because of its lightweight, easy playability, and low cost) is the single horn. Also, it is the most popular choice for beginning students.

The main difference between single and double French horns is the number of valve slides per rotor. In general, single horns have one valve slide per rotor, while double horns have two. Two tubing sets make the double horn heavier and more complicated to use than the single French horn.

These fingering charts are suitable for F and Bb single horns and F/Bb double horns.

While the F single french horn has 3 buttons, both the F/Bb double French horn and the Bb single French horn have 4 buttons, the extra being for the thumb. The numbers of buttons that are colored are those that need to be pressed to play the given note.

You can cut out the charts or use them directly from the booklet. The size of the cut-out is 6.5x10 inches (16x25 cm).

### F/Bb double horn                    Bb single horn

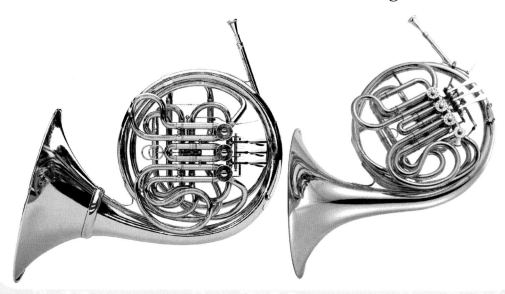

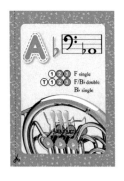

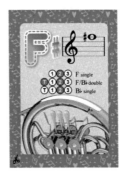

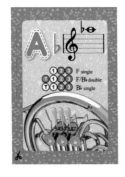

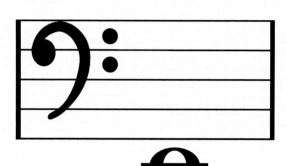

F single

 F/B♭ double

B♭ single

F single

F/B♭ double

B♭ single

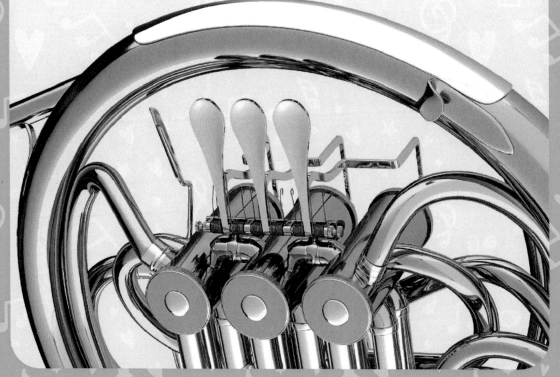

1 2 3     F single

T 1 2 3     F/B♭ double

B♭ single

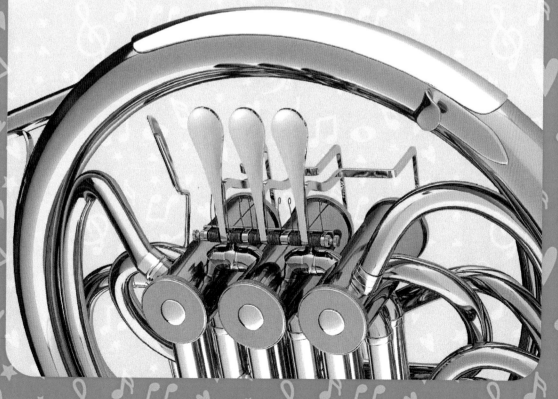

1 **2** 3    F single

T 1 2 3    F/B♭ double

B♭ single

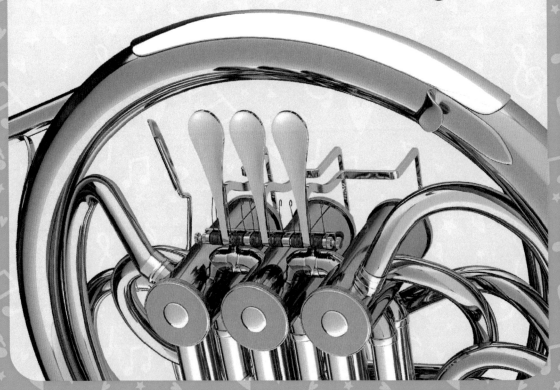

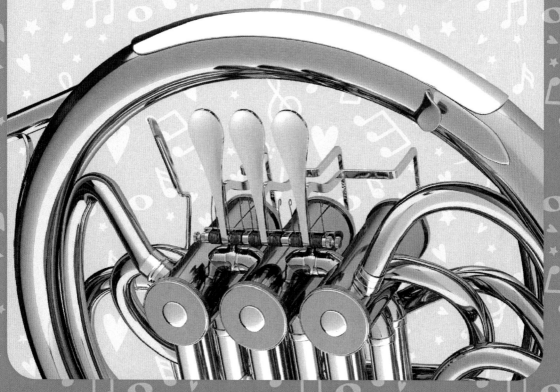

1 2 3    F single

T 1 2 3    F/B♭ double

B♭ single

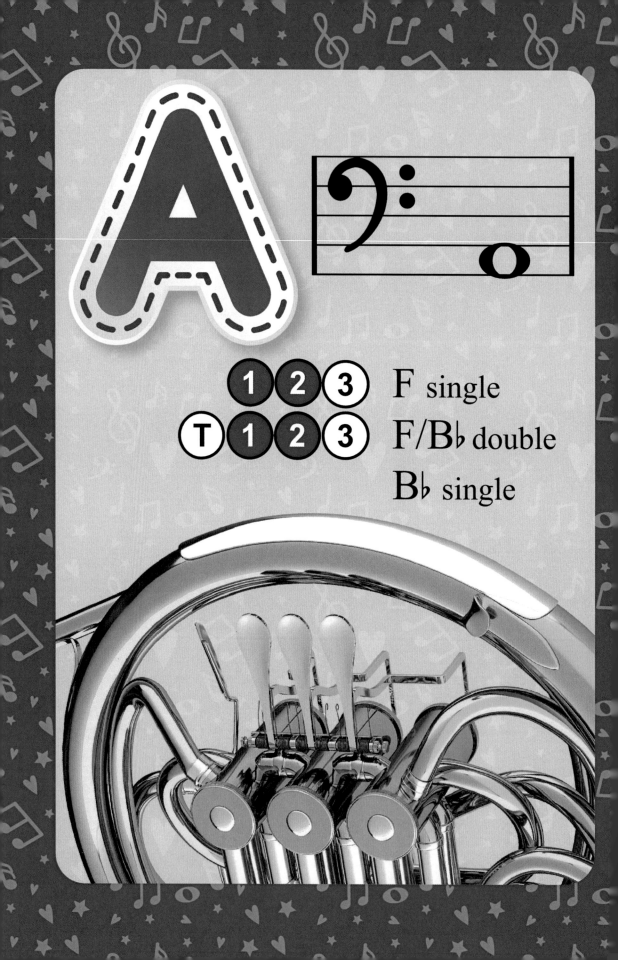

## B♭

1 **2** 3  F single

**T** 1 **2** 3  F/B♭ double

**T** **1** **2** **3**  B♭ single

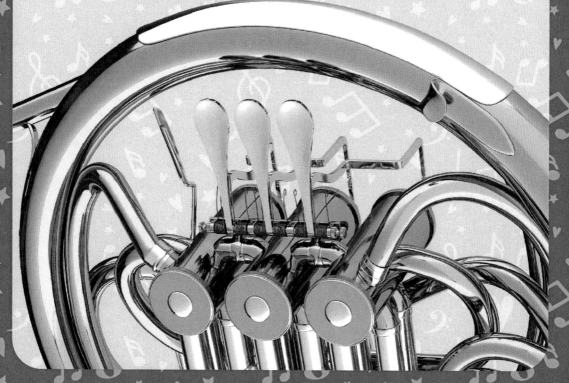

1 2 3    F single

T 1 2 3    F/B♭ double

T 1 2 3    B♭ single

# D

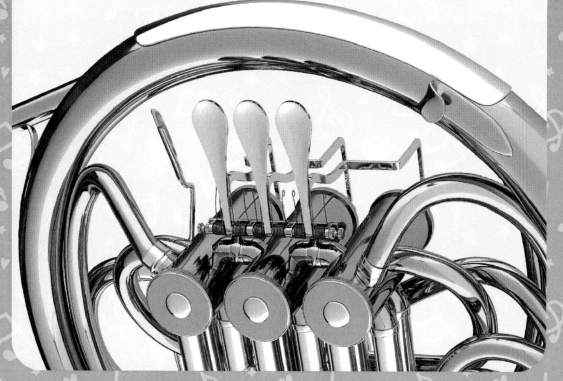

| | | | F single |
| T | 1 | 2 3 | F/B♭ double |
| T | 1 2 3 | | B♭ single |

1 2 3 — F single

T 1 2 3 — F/B♭ double

T 1 2 3 — B♭ single

B♭

| ① ② ③ | F single |
| Ⓣ ① ② ③ | F/B♭ double |
| Ⓣ ① ② ③ | B♭ single |

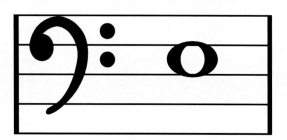

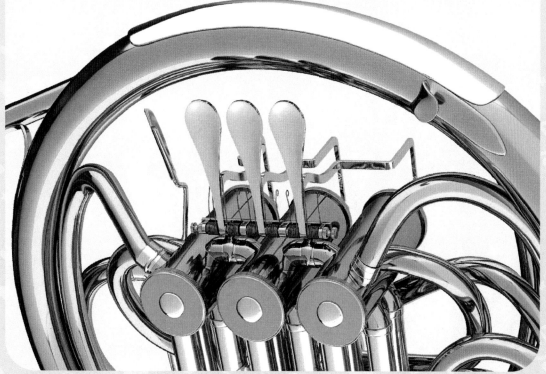

1 2 3 — F single

T 1 2 3 — F/B♭ double

T 1 2 3 — B♭ single

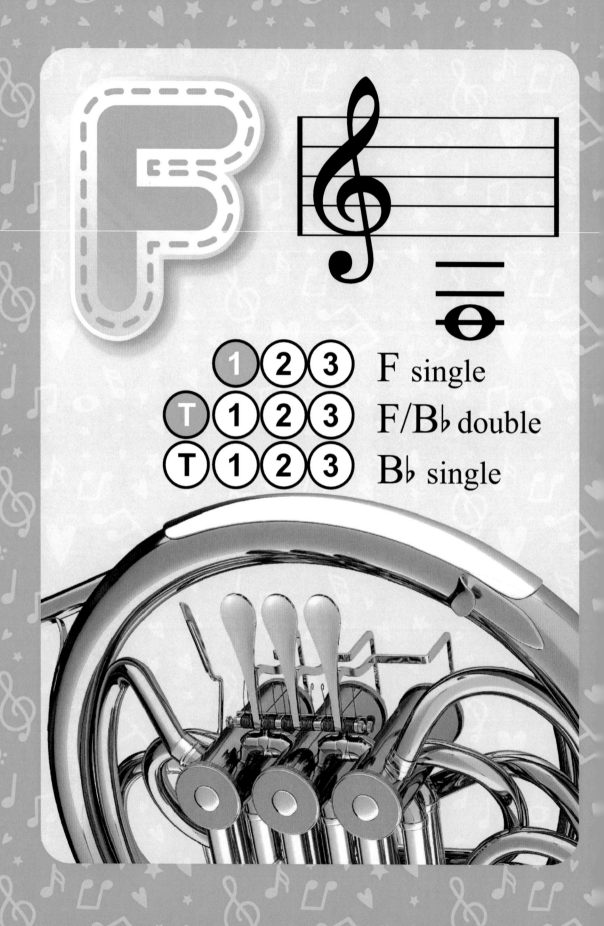

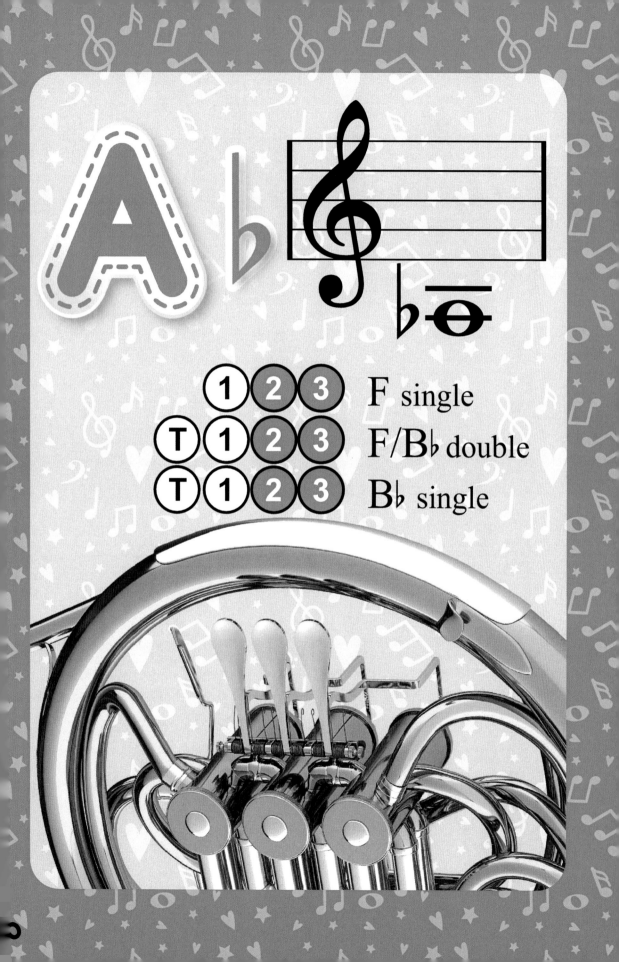

1 2 3  F single

T 1 2 3  F/B♭ double

T 1 2 3  B♭ single

# D

F single

F/B♭ double

B♭ single

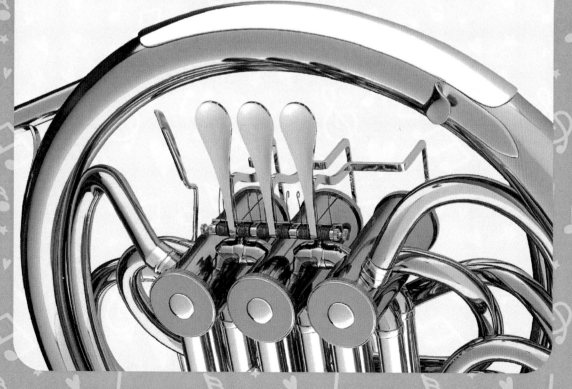

(1)(2)(3)   F single

(T)(1)(2)(3)   F/B♭ double

(T)(1)(2)(3)   B♭ single

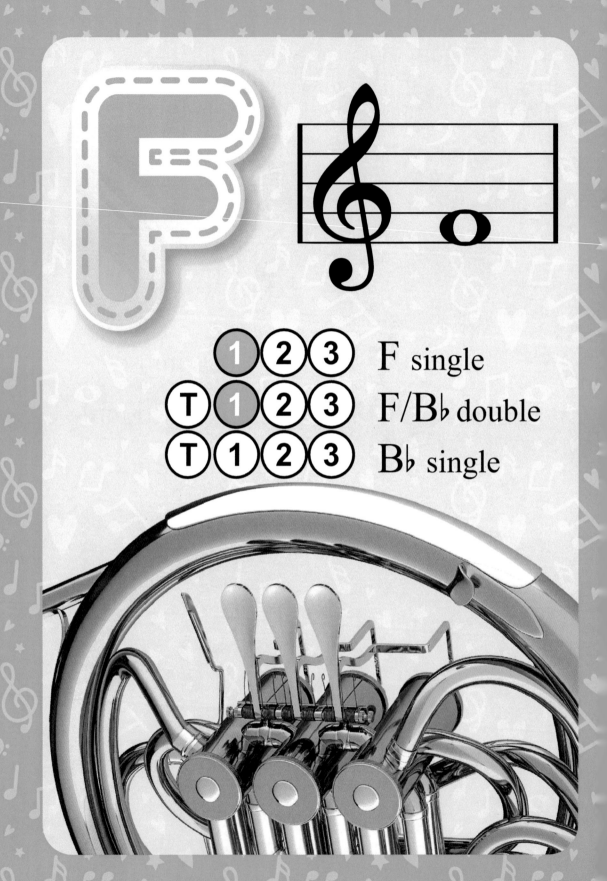

| | | | |
|---|---|---|---|
| 1 | 2 | 3 | F single |
| T 1 | 2 | 3 | F/B♭ double |
| T 1 | 2 | 3 | B♭ single |

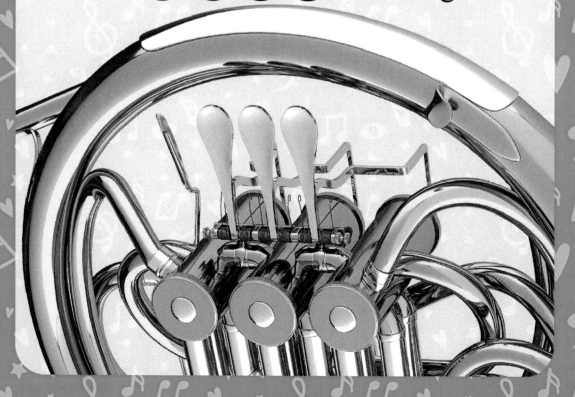

| | | | |
|---|---|---|---|
| | ① ② ③ | F | single |
| T | ① ② ③ | F/B♭ | double |
| T | ① ② ③ | B♭ | single |

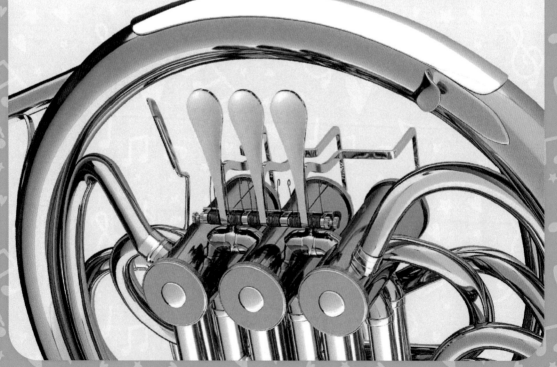

| | | | |
|---|---|---|---|
| **1** | 2 | 3 | F single |
| T | **1** | 2 | 3 | F/B♭ double |
| T | **1** | 2 | 3 | B♭ single |

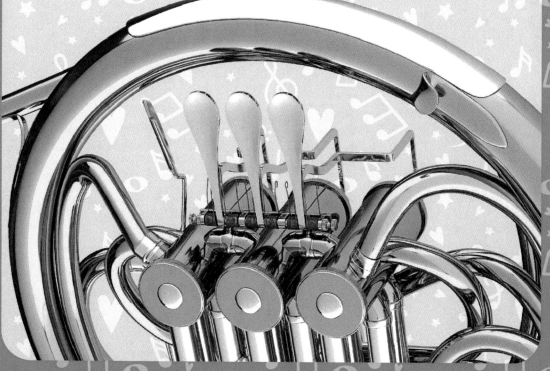

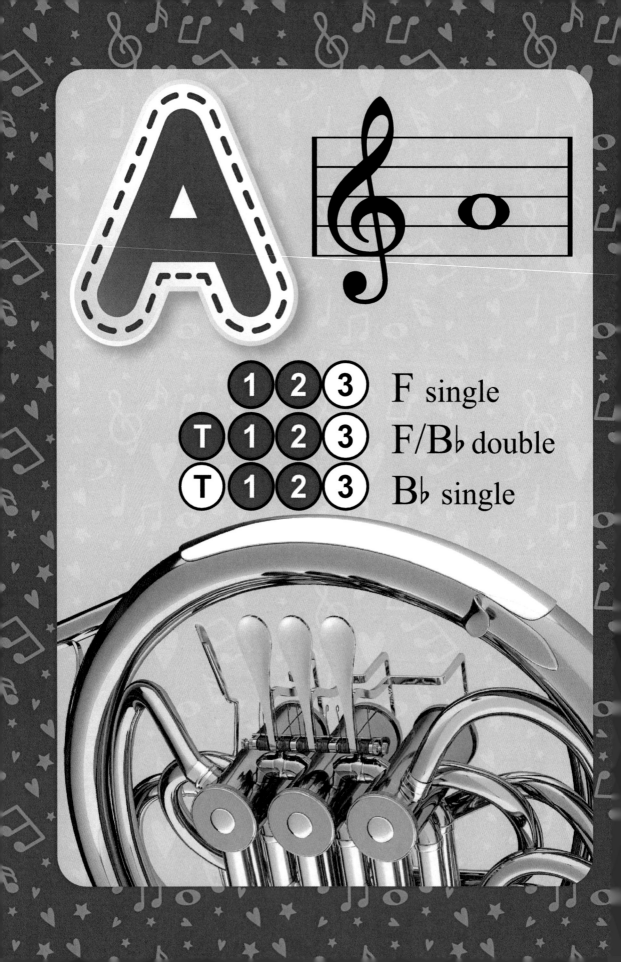

1 **2** 3  F single

**T** 1 **2** 3  F/B♭ double

**T** 1 2 3  B♭ single

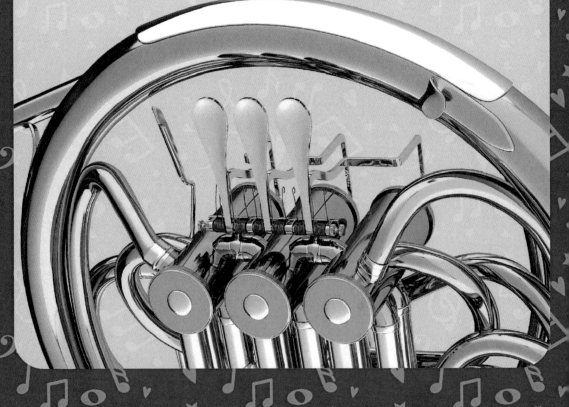

# D

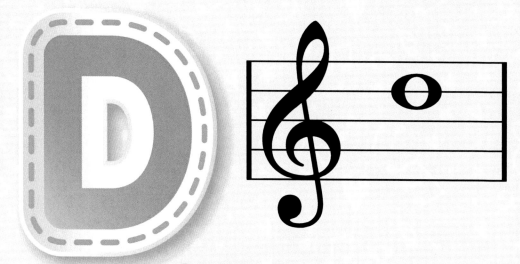

- ① ② ③   F single
- Ⓣ ① ② ③   F/B♭ double
- Ⓣ ① ② ③   B♭ single

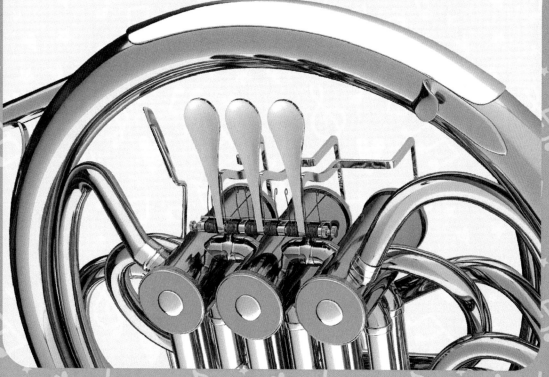

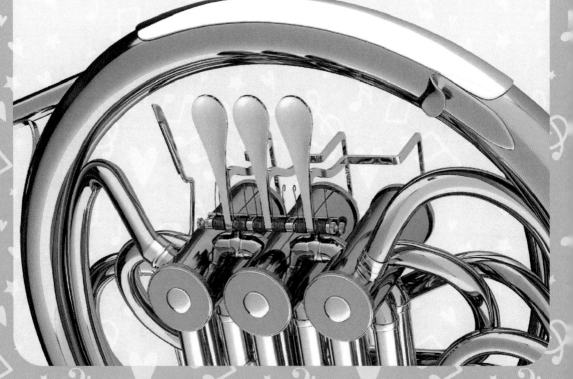

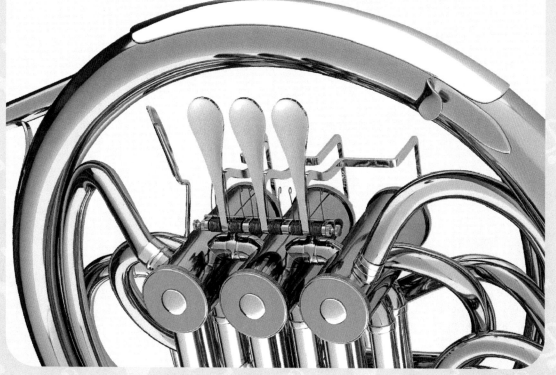

F single

F/B♭ double

B♭ single

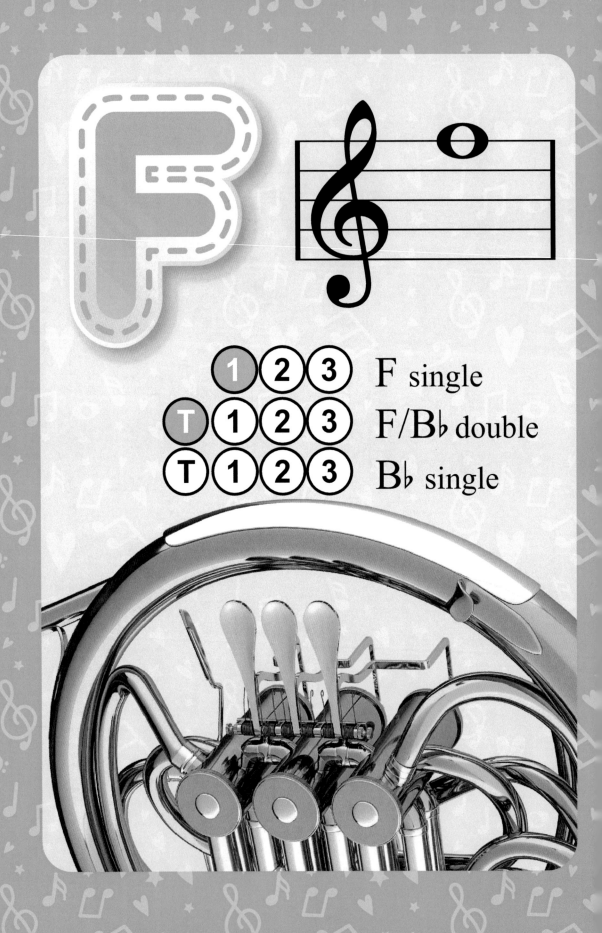

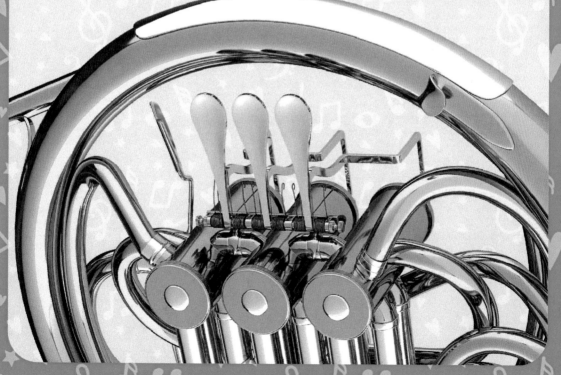

1 **2** 3   F single

**T** 1 **2** 3   F/B♭ double

**T** 1 **2** 3   B♭ single

G

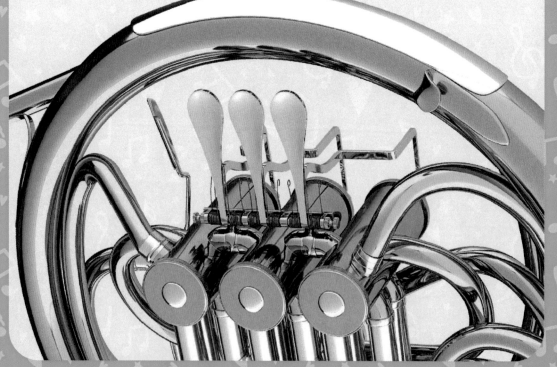

F single

F/B♭ double

B♭ single